CLOUD
PARADIGM

CLOUD PARADIGM

CLOUD CULTURE, ECONOMICS, AND SECURITY.

TONY ADAMS

iUniverse®

CLOUD PARADIGM
CLOUD CULTURE, ECONOMICS, AND SECURITY.

iUniverse books may be ordered through booksellers or by contacting:

iUniverse
1663 Liberty Drive
Bloomington, IN 47403
www.iuniverse.com
844-349-9409

ISBN: 978-1-6632-3293-9 (sc)
ISBN: 978-1-6632-3375-2 (hc)
ISBN: 978-1-6632-3374-5 (e)

Library of Congress Control Number: 2021925409

Print information available on the last page.

iUniverse rev. date: 12/28/2021

CONTENTS

PREFACE

As more and more IT organizations are embracing Cloud to deliver products and service offerings to customers, the challenges remain on some key questions. How do I optimize for agility? How do I design a responsive operating model with a pragmatic security and risk management approach? Most companies have optimized for efficiency for doing what they are able to do for lowest cost. The companies that can quickly transform its culture, can change its bureaucracy, can change its organization and can change its technology architecture, will be successful in the Cloud transformation journey. All parties and stakeholders need to come together to create that organizational agility. The beauty of cloud is that there are many services available for your company to use as building blocks. The cloud unleashes true agility by allowing companies to incorporate cloud services to your IT systems reliably, securely and very quickly. To be successful in the cloud, you need to lead with a Cloud first vision with clear goals and set of plans. Embrace a continuous transformation mindset and take that leap of faith to modernize your architecture that gives you an edge. This book talks about basic Cloud concepts, constructs, patterns and how we should think with product mindset, understand and design our cloud culture which influences our business drivers to solve customers' changing needs.

INTRODUCTION

Welcome to the Cloud Paradigm book! I assume that you are a Cloud practitioner and a thought leader who wants to better understand some of the best practices that would help you navigate your Cloud journey. Help you set the right Cloud culture and transformation. I will discuss some basic cloud constructs, and discuss some best practices that are proven to help cloud adopters. I will also talk about how the cloud is absolutely helping tech leaders to get rid of old tech debts that they have been carrying around. Discuss how Cloud blueprinting mindset and design helps create a repeatable, frictionless DevSecOps process and reinforces leaders to think API (Application Processing Interface) as a product in the border Cloud adoption framework. Two critical topics that interest all leaders are economics of cloud and cloud security. We will touch on those too. Hope you enjoy reading this book.

Cloud Paradigm combines cross domains and disciplines of system administration, software building, database administration and management, network administration and maybe others. All these disciplines work together to build and manage applications that scale up and down though code. Cloud paradigm touches DevSecops practices. It drives a modular building mindset and helps us get away from building closely coupled systems. Cloud paradigm reinforces the thought mindset that we are here to build products and release value quickly to our customers and not worry about owning infrastructure meaning speculating how much infrastructure we will need in future and what is the right investment. Cloud paradigm wins on that argument.

ACKNOWLEDGEMENTS

Special thanks to my graceful mother, who encourages me every day to be humble, kind and have a positive outlook in life.

WHY CLOUD

Cost savings are always fascinating for companies. But that is not just the reason why cloud is so important for companies. Cloud gives companies agility. Cloud offers hundreds of newer technologies and services that allows companies to achieve time to market at a lot faster rate. Companies do not have to build servers, databases, storages and constantly scale them up when there is a high volume of need and when not used, pay for the unused storage, unused compute. A capital expenditure nightmare. With the cloud, companies could provision what is needed, scale up or down seamlessly and get rid of unused resources. A true agility. Leadership commitment to make the move to cloud is critical.

BUSINESS GOALS
AND OBJECTIVES

Industries are being disrupted and the velocity of change has increased significantly. Setting the right business goals and customer focused objectives is key to designing a realistic cloud framework to deliver values to the customer. Cloud encourages that technical sense of agility and helps prioritize companies' investment dollars to change quickly and learn constantly. In order to align with business goals and objectives delivery culture, IT organizations must be optimized for agility and deliver with optimized or lowest cost. That is why the digital transformation is critical. The cloud aligns the agile development culture with DevSecOps, microservices, containerization, serverless technologies and so on. Infrastructure is now a service. Cloud eliminates that waste and reduces the delivery cycle time. That is agility.

RIGHT APPROACH FOR
THE CLOUD JOURNEY

Culture. Leadership. Education. Relentless improvement and love for customers. The need to adapt. All these are right mindsets. Institutionalizing the ability to take advantage of modern technologies creates a competitive advantage. IT leaders must provide the thought leadership to move from a capital investment heavy infrastructure model to "pay as we use" and "don't pay for idle time" model. And that is not just the approach, there is more.

Adopting cloud native architecture provides businesses the agility to release value to customers. It is just not about moving infrastructure, it is about creating an architecture that allows a business to build capabilities securely and fast. Just imagine that your time to market is 60-90% less due to the native cloud technologies. So it goes back to People, Process and Productization.

Leaders must create the urgency, awareness and educate their talents, hire cloud skilled talents and train existing talents with cloud native technologies. Budget for education, training, attending cloud events and conferences. Design a process where the leadership has clear visibility of strategic priorities and how each priority is driven by customer needs. This same process would be flexible enough that we, the organization, is agile enough to pivot anytime if the market is signaling us in a different direction. Redirect resources, tools, technologies that are easy to embrace. That shift a lot of times tells us the maturity of our DevSecOps culture.

Finally, the productization of cloud allows businesses to borrow cloud native technologies and apply into their framework to deliver services. For example, XaaS model means delivering anything as a service. Software, infrastructure, security etc. are part of XaaS model. It allows businesses to focus on changing customer experiences expectations, allows, actually no, rather forces companies to innovate. Technology leaders, armed with productization strategy, are able to assess the potential of their digital assets.

REINVENT THE CLOUD VIA RIGHT MIGRATION STRATEGIES

There is no one-size-fits-all strategy. First the leaders must put some basic framework in place around cross functional teams dedicated to the migration strategies. That also encompasses creation of a "Landing zone". The basics of right migration is still a basic process. Understand the new system, assess gaps in the current system, plan and then do the migration. Cloud migration strategies require understanding the IT asset portfolio, understanding the processes to migrate based on the approaches and then validation. These approaches are well known as "R's". Gartner originally outlined 5 R's in 2011. Later the industry added 1 or 2 more, it just varies. There "R's" are:

1. Retain as do nothing, or these are known as revisit at a later time

2. Retire as get rid of.

3. Rehosting is known as life and shift.

4. Replatforming involves some kind of optimizations to the application during the migration stage. For example, moving from your own relational database system to a turnkey managed RDS on a cloud provider.

5. Repurchase is sometimes referred to drop and shop to move to another product.

6. Refactoring is basically re-architecting. This is usually driven by a strong desire to improve a service or application.

Your migration approaches must be justified by your clear assessment of vision. Why you need to migrate may be driven by the tech debt or even tech skill debt. What I mean by that is that you may want to migrate to cloud as the cloud native are the technologies are something developers are interested to learn and develop skills for. No one wakes up and says, "I want to be a database administrator". The point is that you may not need a formal business case to migrate to cloud. There are a lot of values besides the obvious ones.

Remember, migration is not a simple process. It is complex and proper planning is required. Always ensure you have a good CMDB. I know exactly what you are thinking. Who is up to date with CMDB? No One. So ensure you have collected all licensing, dependencies, architectural data of the applications 1st. Monolithic and mainframes have more complexities than the applications you have built in the last 3-5 years as a rule of thumb. Remember, you want to get a migration framework in place so that you can create patterns for your applications and those 6 "R's" approaches. Start with easy ones and think agile. Think simple. Think scale. Get those cross domain teams in an agile framework and orchestration. Ensure business and product leaders are in those agile teams while everyone is part of the Cloud Center of Excellence.

Let's look into the 6 "R's" and apply some techniques that many companies have learned over time. If you have to migrate quickly, then Rehosting is a good option. There are Pros from this is that you have already migrated the application, data and network. When you are ready to re-architect or modernize these applications, you are already in the cloud. Rehost is not any optimization, rather just the "lift and shift".

Retain is usually "revisit later" or "do- nothing". Usually these are applications that are not a priority to migrate. Retire is another opportunity to assess the portfolio and align with a strategy for the business. Replatforming deals with minor "tinkering" of the application to achieve some benefits but it is not the refactoring or re-architecting. For example, moving a database from on premise to managed services in the cloud lessens the burden of time and cost of managing the database, patching, upgrading, securing etc. Refactoring or re-architecting is where you are truly moving your application into cloud native technologies and features. Remember, you are just not doing it because it is cool to refactor, you are driven by a solid business case that by re-architecting, you are going to achieve scale, performance, adding newer features easily etc. otherwise it would be costly and complex in the existing environment of that application.

This is what I would like to share with you. Between rehosting and re-architecting, re-platforming gives us a middle ground. Also, if you use a big crane to lift all your junk and move from one space to another, that really doesn't give you the value. It carries all your application limitations to a different location. You don't want that either. Flip side, rehosting takes significantly less time and always you should think of automating that process. Get some quick TCO (total cost of ownership) savings in the bank. So, what is the right degree of re-platforming? That is a data driven leadership decision. Create a pattern and strategy for all your applications along with their dispositions.

Here is something to think about. When your applications are already in the cloud, it is a lot easier for you to re-architect and almost redesign your application framework in the cloud. So rehosting has benefits. Think of it as the beginning of a true cloud native approach you are about to embark on. I encourage leaders to always think about re-factoring or re-architecting the applications that enable your business with newer capabilities that cloud native architecture or technologies could help. Reinvention and reimagination happens here via creating performance, scalability etc. Zero trust security in the cloud is also a key topic to think about which I will talk about in a later chapter.

Mainframes could easily be migrated too via re-hosting of workloads or you may do a full blown re-engineering. Sometimes you may need a little bit of replatforming as you may move an older database into a newer RDMBS engines. Re-engineering approach works well when your current mainframe runs its course and no longer supports your changing business needs and business case demands newer architecture of the mainframe. As a cloud leader, you must not execute a strategy where you leave off mainframe workloads. These are part of your strategy and plan.

EXPERIMENT, EDUCATE, LEAD A CLOUD CULTURE

In order to create a culture of experiment, failure must be welcomed and be part of the emotional safety culture. Smart risk taking fosters innovation. In order to be successful, there needs to be executive level support for cloud transformation. Continuous learning and training of the existing talent and hiring talents who bring in outside perspectives is also a key. For any large scale cloud transformation, you will need expert partners, tools providers, system integrators, product configurators. Embrace the hybrid architecture but ensure you're achieving efficiencies, scale and flexibility.

Create a mindset that IT is not a cost center rather an integrated enabler of business capabilities. Provide clear and unambiguous leadership guidance. Ensure the cloud strategy is shared, communicated via all forms of communications mediums and have a feedback loop process in place. More you share, the better and faster your feedback loop helps you do better, avoid mistakes. Be ready to embrace when you hit some bumps.

CLOUD CENTER OF EXCELLENCE

Any strategic vision may have two parts to it. One part is the one that no matter what, you want to be strict and rigid about and that is mission critical. The other part is the one that is ever-evolving and influenced by changing goals. A vision must be created by the Cloud Center of Excellence (CCoE) to mesh best practices, frameworks and governance. Hello CCoE, start small and scale. Put together agile diverse cross domain teams. These are the early adopters mindset people who are excited to improve and iterate. Focus on basics when you are organizing your CCoE. who, what and how.

Who will be the builders? What will the governance look like? What will be the processes and tools? Yes, the evolving budget. Funding mechanisms. Who are the architectural and application teams? Don't forget HR or marketing or any other stakeholders. The teams you want to formulate with have a diverse organizational background. Always ensure you are pulling the entire organization together and people are feeling included. Have a Cloud first and agents of change mindset and strategy. Have some very focused and organized frameworks around roles and responsibilities that you have today mapped with your current organization. Think how you like to organize those in the cloud. Cost structuring is something that always helps sub organizations to understand accounting and cost management aspects. CCoE helps optimize costs for the portfolio. CCoE must put a lot of thought leadership around environments, architectures, business processes and change management too.

DEVSECOPS IN THE CLOUD

Ensure you are focusing on customer journeys and taking everything closer to the customer. See how you could build a practice that supports practices like DevSecOps and culture of automation. Bring those together to create customer centricity. While creating a modular process to deliver the right architectural patterns, Dev and operations must come together. Always build softwares and modernize your tech stack together as one team. Create a culture of transparency and automation so teams are performing efficiently. Building and releasing in production is one seamless co-owned process, not disjoint processes. Foster product mindset with DevSecOps teams. Get into the habit of releasing value as frequently as possible. That forces teams to institute automation and best possible quality checks. Think of scale. Even on a global scale if necessary. Keep that line of conversation and transparency with the business. Build a trusted relationship as partners between IT and Business.

PUTTING MULTI OR HYBRID CLOUD TO WORK

On one hand, most companies are absolutely reluctant to lock themselves in one vendor cloud. On the other hand, architecting and designing an application to work in different cloud vendor platforms beats the entire conversation around taking advantage of cloud native technologies that a vendor may provide to gain efficiency, scale, globality, flexibility etc. Then it becomes more of a how to design my application so it works for multi cloud multi vendor platforms. One smart way to address it is to create applications that are reproducible, modular and highly decoupled from infrastructure. But the more you drill into it, if you ask me, there are a lot of cloud vendor specific technologies once you start to design your application framework with, keeping it multi-vendor, fails to render the optimum cost savings and superior technologies that unleash event driven microservices, zero trust securities, network management, event managements, identify and access management and many more cloud centric technologies.

THE EVENT DRIVEN ARCHITECTURE

As you can understand from the naming of it, events trigger a function between decoupled services. An event could be an update, for example, when you click add to an item to a shopping cart or click on a flight, it is about change in state. Events could also carry information like what items you added to the shopping cart, description, quantity etc. Events can be just as simple as a notification. Interested parties can subscribe to the events or they can also just be published. Event driven architecture, microservices and containerization are technologies that work together in a cloud framework. We will lightly touch these and some more topics just to understand how cloud native architectural patterns have the characteristics to take full advantage of Cloud to scale.

MICROSERVICES

There are a lot of benefits for Microservices. Being independent and modular and scalable are key. Also remember, microservices are designed with a bounded context. Designed correctly, the blast radius can be contained. True microservice should be easily deployable. Cloud allows that decoupled abstraction where your microservices are loosely coupled, distributed and allows scale and resiliency.

CONTAINER TECHNOLOGY

Containers and Kubernetes are two of the leading drivers of digital transformation. Software application containerization makes it easier for developers by abstracting computing infrastructure, and adoption of enterprise container platforms is increasing. By 2025, more than 85 percent of global organizations will be running containerized applications in production, which is a significant increase from fewer than 35 percent in 2019.[1] Containerized architecture allows developers to package software and all its dependencies in portable fashion, allowing the application to run in environments. This container architecture allows defining infrastructure as a code. Very useful as you're defining your microservices framework supporting elasticity and automation.

CNCF (Cloud Native Computing Foundation) defines container technology essential to cloud native landscape. There are tremendous advantages to container architecture. By running many containers on a single virtual machine, you can lower infrastructure costs. You are not constantly scaling VMs or instances as you are achieving scalability by leveraging microservices. Much faster to start and stop a container vs. a VM resulting in faster computation. As long as you have a hist OS, all you need is a container engine on top of the host making the container OS independent. If you want resiliency, you will love containers as you can refresh and redeploy a new container from the same image.

Containers are lightweight, immutable, easily automated and portable. This portability is a lucrative characteristic as you can port a container between environments, data centers and multi cloud environments. Bottomline, have your framework and strategy in place so your application designs are guided by observability, container security practices, disposability of containers and importantly, image immutability.

KUBERNETES

The magic happens here. Beautiful orchestration of your containers. Grouping into logical units allows better discovery, management for containers by this open source technology. Kubernetes is an ecosystem that allows easy creation of container images over VM images. K8 or Kubernetes nicely does the load balancing in case you have high traffic to a container. The self healing mechanism is absolutely to developers' liking, as K8 can restart, replace, or even stop containers that have user defined response issues until they are cured.

PODs and Nodes

Nodes come from worker machines that comprise clusters and they run containerized applications. Application workloads have components named Pods which are hosted by worker nodes. Kubelets is an agent that is running on each node of a cluster. Its job is to make sure that containers runs in a POD.

Docker

Now that we understand a container, we must talk about the open platform name Docker which gives us the ability to run these applications inside containers.

Docker helps the development lifecycle by allowing developers to work in standardized environments using local containers to allow applications and services. Containers are great for continuous integration and continuous delivery (CI/CD) workflows.

Docker enables packaging and running applications in loosely isolated environment named container. The isolation and security allows to run containers simultaneously on given hosts). Containers are lightweight and contain everything needed to run the application, eliminating the need to rely on installations on the host.

Cluster

It is the foundation of Kubernetes architecture. You are running at least one cluster if you are running kubernetes. A simple way to understand is that a container runs on a POD and a group of PODs run on a cluster. Cluster may contain many PODs.

Service Mesh

Microservices are distributed and require smart observability, traffic management, security etc. Service Mesh gives that extra layer of abstracted dedicated infrastructure layer for your distributed application services. It is amazing how Service Mesh can provide discovery, load balancing, failure recovery, metrics and monitoring. Distributed application architecture is based on service to service communications and routing management, across and within application clusters. Proxies route requests between microservices in their own layer. These individual proxies are called "sidecars" in the service mesh as they kind of run alongside and not inside the microservices. This decoupling of proxies from each service makes that mesh network. Now you do not need to code the service to service communications with your logic. Just think of the inefficiencies to troubleshoot a service failure diagnosis as communication logic is abstracted within each service. Not efficient at all.

I won't get into the technical architecture of Service Mesh like control plane, data plane or into Istio, an open source service mesh that layers transparently onto existing distributed applications. Its Uniformity and efficiency helps to secure, connect, and monitor services. But the point is that integrating the Service Mesh architecture into the Blueprint productization creates those efficiencies. More elaborated in the Cloud Blueprint section.

ECONOMICS OF CLOUD

It requires thought leadership. Market sends signals to change and sometimes you have to quickly react to disruptive signals. Cloud provides that versatility with cost efficiency and helps accelerate data and response preparation. Cloud Economics helps switch from capital expenses around data centers and physical servers to pay as you use and not pay for idle time either model. Managed Cloud service providers have perfected the economies of scale and they are running infrastructure as a service for you and providing cloud native technologies a lot cheaper than you trying to do these in your data center. Cloud can provide near real time dashboards to view your usage cost and not only that, it can provide visibility to where more cost savings could be achieved.

The entire Cloud economics model requires a shift from the traditional mindset of capital investment and to continue investing in maintaining and servicing over time. The TCO may consist of Server costs may have facilities cost, space, power, cooling; the storage and network costs may have similar, plus IT labor may have server admin, virtualization admin, storage admin, Network admin, Support team eyc. Then on top, you may have training, cost of capital, legal, project managers. And there may be other costs like upgrades, security, taxes, IT labor like security admins etc. Workforce productivity must always be at the forefront of economics decisions. Leaders must recognize that an on-premise datacenter may be under-utilized. In the old economics model, IT kept asking for money funding to build peak load requirements when there are fluctuations, part time and cyclical (black friday, cyber monday etc.) peak demands and the model is built "to be inflexible". Waste is built into this model. Cloud leaders should drive clarity around capacity (basic metrics on added servers etc, and flexibility to turn servers on and off when not used), utilization (do we over-provision for peak?), what point will we run out of data center space and what is the trend on the data center budget? Equipped with all these data, laser focus on strategies around TCO. Pay for what we use and not for idle time. How to leverage from economies of scale with the managed service providers' offerings? Deep dive into various pricing models and align the optimal plan that supports the business use cases. This is not a one time event, rather build this with governance programs for the cloud. Have clarity on how to optimize costs as you grow bigger and scale further. Cloud elasticity models address a lot of those over provisioning challenges. Deep dive into looking into your usage patterns and make decisions on on-demand, reserved, spot, etc pricing savings opportunities. Have conversations with your managed cloud service providers on the volume tiered pricing discounts.

Now let's peel this even further. Cloud is just not about on premise to Lift and shift into cloud service provider savings. In order to truly take advantage of the cloud's capabilities, as a cloud leader, you should look into instance right sizing, elasticity need and trend, storage optimization, container architecture, serverless architecture so your strategy to refactor or replatform or re-architect is planned well and fits into the Cloud blueprint and framework and guided by Cloud Security and Governance models. Again, I will mention, a lot of tools allow you to measure, monitor. Work with your managed service provider experts on cost optimization improvements.

There are some cheat sheets you can use. Use a high number of smaller instances vs lower number of larger instances. This right sizing and elasticity rule may help lower your cost. On the instance side, as long as it meets your performance and demand needs, feel free to select the cheapest instance. Understand what type of storage class of products meet your usage patterns. Do you need block level storage or low-cost highly durable storage service for long term backup or archival need? Keep all these in mind to achieve cost efficiencies. In your Cloud governance, review what KPI makes sense.

There are a lot of other factors that should contribute to your Cloud Economics thought leadership. Are you planning to go global and how quickly? How to shift your dollar into product development and maturity vs building data centers and running them. Economics go hand in hand with increasing speed and agility, reduction in T2M (Time to market). It is very likely that you may already be in the cloud. Then ask yourself about the right sizing we discussed above, ask yourself about the benefits of reserved instances and do we really need to run our instances 24/7/365? How are we leveraging auto-scaling?

Remember, Cloud economics is a mind shift. It is a culture that needs to be instilled in the people and in the organization who are building and managing the products and product life cycle. Bake this cost optimized architecture into your framework so that DevSecOps teams are embracing Cloud economics at scale mindset in their practice. For a large organization, create a role as Cloud Economics Czar who can steer the stakeholders and broader organization via CCoE and keep Cloud cost optimization framework and discipline dialogs visible.

CLOUD SECURITY
FRAMEWORK

Cloud Security is a vast subject. I will touch on Security best practices and how Security could be baked into the framework that we abstract from the Cloud Blueprinting paradigm we want to build in our Cloud Journey. Security is a shared responsibility. It is not just by the Security Team. Cloud security frameworks must have preventative strategies that allow DevSecOps teams to build applications with agility in the cloud with security first mindset. CCoE must foster a mindset with all cross domain teams that security must be baked into processes, applications, data, network, containers, user identity and access management framework. Meet compliance requirements and standards with the right degree and level of policies. Network protection in itself is a vast subject and teams should design a zero trust security architecture to protect applications and Data. Cloud leaders must think about a programmatic approach to cloud security with a cohesive long term strategy in place. Make it a standard practice to go through a checklist of items like policy, standards and guidelines, Data Ownership, Personal Access, resource provisioning, log management, network security and overall business continuity plan. Develop a cloud security road. Do a gap analysis and assess your security current state and future desired state. As a true cloud leader, think about a "secure-by-design" model for your organization. Security is not an afterthought.

Now, to be successful in Cloud security, build and implement layered security within applications. Cloud first mindset will help enforce you to design decoupled systems even at the component level. That helps with recovery and resiliency.

You know it as a leader, automate, automate and automate. Implement a comprehensive and smart monitoring system. Have the shift "security left mindset". Test for security issues in code build stage. Scan container images. IAM is a big topic in Cloud. Keep in mind that IAM requires a security vision especially if you're dealing with a multi cloud environment. MFA (multi factor authentication) should be part of your authentication requirement.

Part of blueprinting your security framework, ensure you have reference architecture and patterns that take account for application life cycles, container security, Key management services, IP management standards with proper NAT gateway policies. Part of your container security practices, there are best practices around node, POD and Cluster security, implement those and make it part of your blueprint. Data Governance should be part of your Blueprint security framework. Encryption policies for Data should always be baked into your Data governance. Encryption best practices should be enforced. Secure your pipeline and CI/CD workflow. Don't

CLOUD GOVERNANCE

CCoE should lead the Cloud Governance framework to ensure asset deployment, system integration, data security and most importantly business collaboration along with legal, compliance, security and HR are all aboard with Governance Strategy. Several disciplines to lead as a Cloud leader. Cost management, identity, cloud adoption framework alignment, mission critical application management, multi cloud management all are part of the Governance framework. Governance is also a layer approach. Beware of local and geographic or political laws and dynamics. Decide on a distributed governance structure and processes. In order to accelerate your Cloud journey, create a governance framework that enhances your cloud adoption and acceleration framework. Ensure you are watching out for Governance Antipatterns. Have clarity on shared responsibilities between your teams and managed service providers. Momentum is key in Cloud migration. Have readiness and mobilization plans shared and communicated to your teams. Do not assume that since you are going to the cloud, security is already there. Govern in a way, that cost conscious organization is behind the framework.

THE CLOUD BLUEPRINTING

In order to build your netgen cloud capabilities, leaders must utilize CCoE, Have clear strategies and approaches to shift to cloud product construct via blueprinting and automating resulting in mass scale. That mindset incubates emerging technologies and accelerates the blueprint product framework to raise customer centricity culture. Cloud blueprints move the service conversations to application architecture conversations. What are some examples of the blueprints? For example, microservices blueprint, machine language blueprint, artificial intelligence blueprint and more. This product concept is needed for Cloud journey acceleration.

Where to start? Start with Blueprint by identifying all your common architectures across all your app states. Design and engineer those blueprints as infrastructure as code. Instantiate the infrastructure as code blueprints with your open source IaaC Software like terraform or any other.

"Terraform is an open-source infrastructure as code software tool that provides a consistent CLI workflow to manage hundreds of cloud services. Terraform codifies cloud APIs into declarative configuration files." [Source Terraform.io]

Now we are able to produce a fully automated deployment framework in our dev or test environment with an abstraction of a compliance layer which ensures basic requirements are met and are fully governed by Cloud and Cyber security policies. With that, now you have a set of products across your blueprints offering compliance, security and control that are baked in. A new DevSecOps member can come and ready to take the blueprint and their architecture framework is already solved for. Benefits are abundant for making a blueprint as a product even for your chaos services. Framework a SaaS chaos where a blueprint like micro services compliance and seCurtis are built in and could be checked by Sentinel or any autonomous Security platform to ensure resiliency requirements are met.

Cloud leaders must ask a fundamental question to themselves. How could we create a product model that supports line of business with a reusable optimized framework? How could we create, manage and optimize workloads at scale with the right level of governance, control and simultaneously provide self service autonomy for the DevSecOps teams.

To further drill down that productization of the blueprint conversation, let's take an instance of a blueprint like micro services. Think of the basic necessities like application load balancer, elastic container registry, EC2 etc. You may add another layer of additional efficiency or automation capabilities lIke Service Mesh or Istio allowing service discovery, fault tolerance, secure connection with TLS, traffic routing and zero downtime deployment. All these create extra efficiency and agility.

Another efficiency framework to your POD permission based on POD identity which allows to map identity into your kubernetes RBAC (Role Based Access Control) configuration.

The point of all these Blueprint mindset shift architectural considerations is that baking these efficiencies into the blueprint creates significant efficiencies for your DevSecOps teams and allows them to scale. Blueprint as products, that is the framing of design where you should capture the bounded context with services in mind and bake them into that blueprint. Another granular abstraction of the blueprint is that peel several layers to create further innovation into the blueprint design. The foundational layer could easily capture your roles, groups, policies and encryption etc. A layer above you could have your network architectural patterns with VPN, Virtual gateway, VPC, subnets, route tables etc. Design another layer of Platform above this where you have ELBs, static data storage, data platforms, security groups etc. Now that you have all these nice abstracted "layers" of the product designed, you are ready to design your product layer which is your core blueprint. You have all your application architectures and framework with bounded context with container, Auto Scaling, Compute instances etc. This layer is built leveraging the other layers.

The big advantage of this layered blueprint approach is that it allows modular configuration, loosely coupled and reusable architecture. It promotes DevSecOps teams to be modular and agile. Now that we have a clear understanding of this shared responsibility model, we can automate and apply Git Ops best practices. The next step is to ensure you have a solid operational framework that will leverage DevSecOps

You now have a version 2.0 product that already has vpc 1.0, eks 1.0 with some configurable options within their product.

Once terraform (replace whatever your IaaC software/ platform is) is configured, you can do your jenkins, set up the pipeline that will run and remote backend into terraform or your open source infrastructure software platform which is configured in the "microservices" [one blueprint] 2.0 product. Then terraform will pull that plan down and see eks 1.0 is there, vpc 1.0 is there, it will see what other private version registry it depends on, configurations are done. Then it will run the sentinel (AI powered Cloud workload protection platform) (or any comparable products like GitHub / Coverity / Checkmarx / Appknox / SonarQube that you may have integrated with your platform to do the policy checks. So we just baked all the policy checks into the product and when those policy checks pass, it will actually provision the infrastructure. We just created an immutable infrastructure, with governance, with compliance with all the useful features that the engineer needs and deployed that into microservice. Microservice Blueprint product.

So now, if we discover an issue, we make that change once, we publish that into the private model registry and all the teams, all the workloads depending on the version will upgrade to the newer version. We just managed to publish massive changes across the enterprise just by managing our blueprint as a product. It is very powerful as it truly allows us to scale up migration to the cloud, allows agility but ensures we have an opinionated architecture that has right security, compliance and controls baked into the cloud.

SUMMARY

Journey to the cloud is more of a business and cultural transformation than it is about technology adoption. Leaders must have a vision and clarity where they like to see themselves now and in future. What the capability landscape would look like. How scalability, flexibility and security can be baked into their cloud architecture and blueprint product mindset is the key. These organizations have figured out a way to reiterate innovations and optimize and reuse their architectural patterns. Layered Blueprint product design with customer centricity, modularity, DevSecOps teams working together with shared responsibility incubates that nextgen Cloud first innovation and sustainment. Cloud leaders should build and foster that innovation culture.

REFERENCE

1. [Reference: As per IBM publication regarding "Kubernetes and Containers Are Leading Drivers of Digital Transformation" https://newsroom.ibm.com/2021-07-08-IBM-to-Acquire-Premier-Hybrid-Cloud-Consulting-Firm]

2. North Texas Book Bank website https://ntfb.org/wp-content/uploads/2021/09/FY21-By-The-Numbers.pdf https://ntfb.org/about-us/our-impact/

Printed in the United States
by Baker & Taylor Publisher Services